THE ANIMAL GOSPELS ::

The Animal Gospels

Brian Barker

02 NOV 2006
murray, ky

For Martin & Patsy —

With great admiration. Thanks
for your warm welcome.

All good things,
Brian Barker

Tupelo Press
Post Office Box 539, Dorset, Vermont 05251
(802) 366-8185
(802) 362-1883 fax
editor@tupelopress.org
www.tupelopress.org

Cover and book design: Josef Beery
Cover photo and calligraphy: Josef Beery

For my parents,

&

for Nicky—
my wind, my light

CONTENTS

FLOOD

(Houston, Texas, 2001)

Where have all the night tunes fled?

The thrum of locusts, those tin blossoms I loved
To hear ratchet and uncoil
                              and swivel down from the cypress trees,
Are long gone, gone with the freight trains
Slogging through the humidity,
                              their shadowchurn over
The tarred trestles, their castanets of wood and air and steel.

And the distant drone of the diesel rigs
Unspooling like bolts of muslin over the rooftops;
And the faint winglisp of Japanese beetles
Coasting the open window,
                              rappelling up the wall,
Dizzy for that place where the light sprouts—

All of it gone, the night's music silenced
And sluiced through the oily gutters,
Into the yawning storm drains clotted
With trash and mud and drowned birds.

Gone and irretrievable, like a few stray eyelashes
Shed by a nightswimmer
                              diving through the dark into darker water.

::

City of forgotten history, where are your dead?
What locks has the rain picked? What dark is this
That silences your cylinders, clicks shut
Your six black moons?

So much undone and rising,

The water thighdeep and spreading like iodine,
Scything the manicured lawns, jostling the shotgun shacks,
Rattling the irongates and razorwire.
Rising over the capsized dumpsters,
Over the little-league fields and playgrounds,
Over the jukeboxes and convenience stores and hospitals,

While the poor ride their flimsy housing
                                down like sheetrock dinghies.

And the homebound traffic submerged,
Frozen in orbit on the interstate
Where the radios warble and bleed beyond earshot.

And the light we hold onto growing cold.

And the light slipping piecemeal below the surface,
This fluid scaffolding, these ghostly constellations

Blurring out of reach beneath the water.

::

It's the rain that calls me out and the night
That anchors me here like a stone.

The night, impenetrable, a layer of charcoal
Sheeting the bottom of a water purification tank.

The night and the silence beneath water.
The silence that we're all being swept towards.

Who will remember us? What will I remember?

Once, when I was sixteen and death didn't exist,
When it didn't follow me as it does now,
This thin, persistent whine behind my left ear,
I shucked my clothes beside the tracks,
Stumbled across a soot-glazed trestle,
And listened to the pigeons rustle on the ledge
As I spread my arms to summon the dumb-luck
And know-not-what that got me there.

I stood on the edge of some undefined space
Where trees, washed in adrenaline,
Ceased to be trees, and the single blue feather
That floated down in front of me,
Just out of reach, held the only light

I thought I'd ever need. When I jumped
The water was no longer
Water, but a doorway, and words a mere
Afterthought filling the room my body carved
In its headlong tumble.

If I could, I'd plunge again into that weightlessness.
I'd shake this undertow from around my ankles
And sink to where the salamander skulls
Lisp their sandy refrains, where the leeches lurk
Among crack pipes and tires and stray shoes.
There where the fire ants refuse
To die, their bodies rising like bubbles
Through the murky corridors.

4 :

I'd follow the water moccasins and catfish,
Gather the coins tarnishing
In the gator mouths and swim to the concrete's edge
Where sewage and gasoline scallop the pylons,
Where the names of lovers
Are scrawled in the shadows and the homeless cling
To cardboard signs. If I could,

I'd hollow their words out and drag the lost
Faces up from the depths.
But the flood's erased the shore, smeared
The messages like octopus ink.

And somewhere behind the clouds
The stars remain, igniting the dark's amnesia.

::

From the driveway's edge, I watch the water
River the street,
           sliding and eddying past,
Rising at the intersection where it boils
Into a gluttonous gray-foam,
Biting at the stopsigns and telephone poles,
Spitting its flotsam out, its scum and bones.

Two Mexican boys drift by on the current
In a dead-man's float, shirtless, their bodies
Dark as skates. Just as they pass,
They roll over onto their backs
Laughing before they hit the spot where the rapids
Begin to wheel and surf out of sight.

And all night I'll worry up the stunned
Rattlesnakes, the uncorked manholes,
The water's chemical sheen and the silence
Swimming like an endless wind beneath.

And all night I'll worry their names
Out of the rain.

I could launch a thousand newsprint boats
Into the eye of the storm to bless them,
Fill the hulls with brand new pennies
To grant them luck. I could climb the trees
With my plastic lantern and light their way,
There where the leaves whisper
Into the night's tincan.

::

I lie in bed a long time before drifting
Into sleep, listening to a helicopter
Circling the city, to the silence that lifts
Like a broken buoy inside its whop.
6 : With my eyes closed I can almost imagine
The faint sound of its spotlight sliding
Over the water, over the mirrored facades
Of the skyscrapers. A sound as precise
As a broom sweeping the linoleum floor
Of the barbershop at closing time
When the barber is alone.
He finishes, removes his smock
And stands smoking, watching the news
On an old television. The gray dusk
Has softened the lines on his face,
Just as it's softened the chrome chairs

Behind him and the headlights of the cars
On the interstate going nowhere now
And the curses of their drivers. Soon
They're pushing the doors open with their feet,
The water and the night pouring through,
Indistinguishable, filling the floorboards
In one funneling gasp, the way grain
Swirls and spills from a silo
Into the sunlight and dust of summer.
Although they never describe it as such
To the bystanders and reporters.
It happened so fast, they say, shivering.
It happened so fast... I hardly remember anything.
And the barber, believing their words
Are already rain and broken glass,
Clicks off the set and turns to the window,
Watching the drops weave and thread
The letters of his name, his face blank
As he stares past everything
Trying to remember what it is he's lost.
What could I say that he won't already understand
When he finds himself standing alone
In the dark, listening to the wind come again
And again, the rain running off
The awning, the sound of water rising?

::

A dream of flood in the midst of flood.

The water goes where it wants and I follow it
Through the drowned streets and alleys,
Through greased cavernous canals of parking garages,
Through unhinged doors and shattered windows,
Up elevator shafts and down hallways.

Telephone lines fishtail and fizz.

Dead letters ride up
                out of the blue breath of mailboxes.

In a hospital basement, cages bob like lobster traps,
The shaved pink bellies of rats bloating
Against the wire mesh, the bright tips
Of unsheathed syringes
                snicking a code against steel and glass.

Somewhere a lone cello floats calmly
Across a playground of my childhood,
As if the world had never known its music,
As if it had never been anything else
But an empty boat. It docks against

The top of a swingset where crows roost,
Lifting their faces into the wind.

What I remember is water and then
No water, the earth spongy
                                        as I kneel beneath
The swing, beside the hole scooped out
Long ago by my gliding feet.
There in a shallow pool tadpoles
Squirm in the mudsuck, hundreds of black
Commas I cup in my hands and carry
To the bank of the swollen creek.

I wait a long time for the cries of their kind
To rise from the rocks and crushed grass.

                    ::

Dawn, and the first sunlight in days,
Mustard-pale and seeping
Through the last of the broken storm bands
Scudding west like a fleet of ashy rafts.

I open the window and the morning air's
Steeped with the smell of mold,
Sewage, rotting fish, and something
Unidentifiable: thousands of mosquito eggs

Taking root in the mud, perhaps,
Or the musky scent of night crawlers writhing
In blind ecstasy on the sidewalk and in the grass.

I could say, *now is the time to start over.*
I could say, *now is the time to pick up the pieces
    and move forward,*

But some good soul says it and means it
When the smoky rasp of a chainsaw
Flares up and ricochets
Through the narrow spaces between homes,
And then the deep, intermittent
Chortle of a generator and pump, and the whine
Of an outboard in the distance
Ferrying people and pets and supplies.

I want to say, *this is the music of beginning again,*
When a face on the news stops me.

It's a Mexican man I've seen somewhere before,
Perhaps slinking in the long sheetmetal
Shadow of the day labor office off Shepherd,
Standing now on the steps of his house,
The street swollen with water and debris.
He's holding a fishing net

And scooping up a muddy wedding dress
Billowing in the backwash of the bayou.

He stands holding it for a long time,
Watching the water empty out
Of its lace skirt and bodice. He doesn't look up,
Not even when the reporter thrusts
The microphone beneath his chin.
He stands staring at the dress,
And before I can speak I'm gone with him
To the place where he last remembers it,
Unzippered and crumpled at the bottom of a skiff
Shored where the cattails bow along the bank,
A half-mile down river from the wedding feast.

: *II*

The stars never so close and silent as this,
As he and his new wife swim, the water
So black and warm against their bodies the world
Seems to be springing forth
For the first time out of the dark,
Out of their footprints pressed in silt,
Out of the willowroots and stones and snakegrass.

And when I study his face
And close my eyes now, I can see the rowing
Back, the oars rising and dripping
Like wet wings. I can feel the hot blisters swell

On my hands and welcome them.
I can hear the music that floods the night
And blesses the boat, and there is
No reason to speak, no reason to say anything.

::

*In June of 2001, tropical storm Allison dumped twenty-eight
inches of rain on Houston, Texas in twelve hours (thirty-six
inches in five days). The storm resulted in one of the worst floods
in American history and was responsible for twenty-two deaths
and five billion dollars in property damage.*

∷

GOSPEL WITH LION
& GAZELLE

This the hour of sweet nothing
when the summer sun spins at the end

of its rope, and the heat leans
against the door, presses its damp

palms all over the window.
This the hour when deadlines fade

and the dogs know no masters
but their breath and sleep, curled

in dark glyphs on the cool floor.
I could lie here with you forever

in these shadows of shuttered day,
in this quiet moment after sex,

my body glad to be broken,
floating like a bubble in amber.

Drape your hair over my chest
and let me smell the dust that clings

to the hooves of fleeing gazelles.
Remind me of the time

when we were yoked
to the small light inside a stone,

when we lay touching each other
until dusk cupped our faces

like the soft mouth of a lion,
and the stars banked and burned

down the sky in the west,
tattooing the backs of the unnamed.

Stay with me here in this space
before speech, where the wind

swallows our cries, maps our bodies
with the salt of the living,

as we hold one another, lost
in this forest of beginning.

::

For Nicky Beer

SELF-PORTRAIT WITH A BURNT OUT LIGHT BULB

Domestic workhorse,
little bastion of incandescence,
how you surprise me

with your unannounced
flaring out, the fizz and flash
of your spent filament,

burnt tungsten showering
faintly in your belly.

This morning it happens

in the bathroom,
your dime-store pyrotechnics
enough to startle me

beneath my thick cloak
of sleep, my bemused face
reflected briefly in the mirror,

an eerie daguerreotype
of some foggy-eyed stranger,
some long-lost pioneer,

wagon-wrecked and wandering.
The window brims
with the milky-blue dark

of dawn, as I unscrew you
blindly from your rusty socket.
Your fragility implies

your violence — scattered
shards, sudden jaggedness.
But I prefer to think

of an egg I hollowed as a child,
my warm breath threading
the barely visible pinholes,

or of a gray-green pear
wobbling on a plate at dusk.
Smoky globe, how long

have I stood here, the ghosts
of buffalo drifting through me,
a black wind in my bones?

How many lives have I lived
just to weigh your cold
nothingness in my palm?

I'm holding you up to my ear
in the dark. I'm listening
for your scarce, peculiar song

of broken light.

ELEGY WITH A MUTE BELL

1.

This is what I've chosen
to remember her by. Not her cabinets
of chipped china, or shelves of porcelain

bric-a-brac, or boxes of empty snuff tins,
but a small bell. The carved handle painted
green, and where the green has given way

to the pinch of fingertips, worn by oil
and salt, the wood shines, rubbed
to a sheen of blackened honey.   : *19*

Its mouth, once a polished silver, is now
mottled with rust, the deep umber
of a softening pear, and when I lift it

only the lip-scrape and hollow clink
of the clapperless tongue: a corroded wire clip
plumbing the bell's vaulted dark.

2.

Imagine what she must have thought
when she picked it up during the night
to beckon the nurse, expecting the perfect

high-toned pitch to shimmer over the sound
of the rain dripping from the eaves.
What she must have thought when the bell

let go of its lead bob, and it fell
for the first time since being drop forged,
hitting the pine floor and rolling—

not the slow, measured roll of the marbles
she played as a girl, but syncopated, skipping,
wobbled by the soldered eyelet—

into a black abyss of safety pins and dust.
What she must have thought when she caught
herself still waving the mute bell like a wand

and knew she was also disappearing, her body
receding into itself, slipping behind her clavicle,
her rib cage, into unseen fissures of light.

3.
It rests on my windowsill, unrung,
yet upright in its silence. I'm certain
if I lifted it, its absence would be marked

on the sill, a black ring, an imprint in the paint.
A bell in form? Yes, but something else,
memory's icon or monument. Or a prop

on a stage, the backdrop this: late afternoon,
the sun's gold delirium against the glass,
the tiger lilies bowing their orange-cowled heads;

the trellis brocaded with roses, and skirting the fence,
a bramble of blackberries, the ripe fruit glistening
like the small things we lose everyday

made palpable again. Starlings swoop from the maple,
snatch the berries, return to their claver and chaos.
They appear iridescent, fat, the berries hardening

in their bellies like ballast. Without warning,
the conclave rises, veers, scatters. They go silent,
grow dark as ink, and before disappearing,

tumble in failed shapes across the sky.

::

Dedicated to the memory of my great-grandmother,
Charlotte Marshall Lowe, 1899-1982

SNOW OVER SHAVERS FORK

Rhododendrons droop
                under the white weight of winter,
and the highway-blue suspension bridge, a lacquered mesh of ice,
turns to milk-glass
                in the slow pan of a pick-up's single headlight.

Tonight, not even the river avoids indifference, as it churns
deep in its groove,
                from here to there and back again,
flashing its eggshell palms in the icy wallow.

Duped again by the silence,
                  by the undertow that drags the slate sky down
to the tips of the pines, by the mountain's chalk-blur shifts,
by the snow bogging down, speechless
                syllables claiming a void—

I know this of the fleeting world: the falling down,
    not the rising up,
the snow persisting in its silence,
                and my hands too human to hold it.

DOG GOSPEL

When I dare at last to imagine hunger,
I see a farmer wandering his parched fields
not knowing what to do, finally, but sleep
the day out in the barn's long shadow,
dreaming of the family dog he drove
deep into a neighboring county
and abandoned by the side of the road.
Weeks later a boy finds it in a ditch —
timid and gimp, a halo of gnats
festering between its swollen testicles
and wormy flanks — and he coaxes it
into some pines, tethers it with a tentstake
and a chain as the late summer light
spirals and drapes over the branches,
a mirage the dog slavers and snaps at.
Consider the boy's amusement
as he imagines the animal jerking the light
down and the ruckus of bells that clang
and catapult from the treetop belfries,
the canopy rent like a piñata, spilling licorice
and circus peanuts, coins and fluttering dollar bills.
The real possibilities are beyond him.
The dog as a parable of pain or loss.
Hunger as some small iridescent thing at work
inside the animal, hovering around its heart
the way a lone dragonfly skirts the dry pond crater,
dismantling the day — light unstitched

from dust, dust unbuckled from air.
By now, the dog's given up, and the boy
watches its tongue loll in the pine needles,
the heave and fall of its stomach, its eyes
following birdflight in and out of the shade.
Restless for something he cannot name,
he imagines the music he might make
if he thumped the dog's belly like a drum.
Imagines its eyes are the color of iron.
Imagines the unimaginable and does it,
the tire tool and the belly unwilling instruments,
and the dog's caterwaul is not like music
at all and when night comes the cricketsong
dulcifies nothing, the dog's body

is just a body, is not paltry, is not glorified.
What hunger is this that haunts the boy,
that haunts the man sleeping in the shade?
Watch as the dragonfly dips into his open mouth
and keeps going, a blur between bone and sinew,
a wet thread collapsing soft caverns of flesh,
gone to where his body is a field
honed by sleeves of sunlight,
to where the boy ceases to be and the man wakes.
He knows what flits through him now
keeps the time with its thrumming,
carrying him away from himself
into himself, to where the dog roves in the shadows —
ravenous, luminous — its tail bobbing
in the heat, a winnowing sliver of light.

THE TREES OF THE SOUTH

Deadfall and new growth, trees of the past
sunk in red clay—
the Japanese cherry that flared
like an Easter boutonniere, and the scraggly
mimosa where a crow perched once,
flashing a quarter in its beak.
Or that stand of pines you raced through,
where her dress snagged on bramble
and buck brush, where soft needles spread
a gentler earth above the earth.
Magnolias, their coppery bangle,
their waxy blossoms drinking up the light,
the finest in a cemetery in Richmond
where all summer scholars drowsed
with musty books tenting their chests,
thirteen thousand crosses
fluttering behind their eyelids.
The gnarled roots of the live oak
that churned the courthouse steps back to dust
as the old laws vanished into the night's vault,
turning backwards on wind and rain
to leaf, to pulp. And the sweet gum in Selma
battered by shotgun blasts,
the cottonwood somewhere outside Charleston
with a foot of rotted rope still dangling
from a branch. There, where the cicadas

climb their wire ladders of song,
and the frantic shadows scissor in the wind
like the arms of a man
flagging down help roadside;
there, where the forest runs out of breath
and the light breaks so suddenly
you have to shut your eyes.

GUINEA PIG GOSPEL

(Tuskegee, Alabama)

Out of mildewed files, out of charts
burnt by the blind god of Indifference and Mistakes,
out of a tainted petri dish and a drawer
strewn with syringes, I rise tonight
and sail on my paper robe
to where the stethoscope's cold drum
hovers over the taut chests of the sleepers.
Honorable Delegates of the Council
on Ends and Means, take note of me now.
Once upon a time I was young and poor.
I laughed. I dreamed. I danced.
I slept naked in a field listening to bullfrogs
bark in the distance, while my blood
coursed the length of my fingerbones
and pounded against my skull, my neck, my heart.
What foolishness, you think.
What dogs did I wallow with, you wonder.
It is true. We are all only human,
and I have paid the price of a multitude,
of my race, of the sick and exploited, of my children
born in the gray muck of my illness
and buried beneath the blighted oak behind the smokehouse.
Ladies and Gentlemen, here is Exhibit X,
my body the bacteria infiltrated,
little flotillas colonizing flesh and blood.
Here are the smoldering chancres, the rashes
that rose then flared out like cities,

sprawling into the suburbs the doctors returned to each
   evening.
They slept in clean beds and their silence
filled windows and closets, bathtubs and sinks,
spread over lawns and spilled into the streets,
drifted up through pines to the stars
that glistened like sugar pills, to the moon
lacquered with the sweat of my fever,
its icy beam smoking on roofs that could be anywhere.
Here is the cure locked away in a cabinet
without a key, marked with a label
I could not read, a warm square of sunlight
that never touched my forehead.
Here are the guinea pigs that ate and got fat
and rolled in cedar chips, left to their fate,
and the delirious swine I carried with me
to death, thrashing against the walls of my body,
the fortified hold of a ship.
And here is my spine, a broken ladder of light
on the floor of the sea that swells
and rages in each of us,
our passage not over, but just begun.

::

*In 1932, 399 African-American men living in rural Alabama signed
up with the U.S. Public Health Service for free "medical care."
The service was conducting a study on the effects of syphilis on the
human body. The men, who were mostly uneducated and illiterate,
were never told they had syphilis. Instead, they were told they had
"bad blood" and were denied access to treatment even after penicillin
came into use in 1947. By the time the study was exposed in 1972,
twenty-eight men had died of syphilis and 100 others were dead of
related complications.*

CROW GOSPEL COMING DOWN
FROM THE MOUNTAIN

In the winter of 1980, when the landfill
Was bulldozed over, the crows strutted into town
To roost in the trees along Beaver Creek
And spar over the trash bins on State Street.

The mountain shone a pale gray-purple,
The color of a crushed crocus,

                or the dying skin of a god

Who turned his back on our town, the double-wides
Sinking in a field of mud, the dim housing projects
With Christmas lights twittering in windows, their chimneys
Scrawling the sour smoke of whatever might burn.

Defeat smelled like a lumbering feathered mustiness

Something vinegar-breathed —

It sounded like the dozens of rusty *caws* that swung
Down through branches, through telephone wires
And television antennas

The day Little Jimmy Jenkins and his ilk, white-robed,
A few of the men playing instruments,
Zig-zagged towards City Hall.

I saw it from the second floor of my elementary school
After someone shouted *Parade!* and the windows filled
With waving, giggling third graders.
                                    Mrs. Rutherford tried to shoo us
Back to our desks, then finally gave up, wrote *freedom* on
    the board
And smoothed out the front of her dress, waiting

For the clangs and squeaks, for the thin
Backs of the men and their sharp, shiny hats
To whittle away in the winter wind.

                    ::

That winter, when the wind tumbled down the dark,
I slept
        and took it all inside me—

The mountain looming in my bedroom window,
Covered in ice, its light waning
From within, daub of leafrot and foxfire going under,
Black branches clicking like turnstiles—

And the crows in the pines behind the Piggly Wiggly
Speaking in tongues, spread-winged and gaff-eyed
When they kited down through snow to the dumpsters—

And Jimmy Jenkins, and Mrs. Rutherford wiping chalk
From her hands, and my parents whispering

About the black and white couple who moved in
    down the street.

Winter wind on my neck, flashback and backlash
Of the past, it all whorls inside me —
                            the Christmas decorations
Downtown, bells and the jostle of bright lights,

Shopping at JCPenneys with my mother
When the battered Job Corps bus sputtered up
And a line of black men filed off,

Dirty and exhausted from working
Construction the whole day, dynamiting

And bulldozing a hole that would become, by summer,
The Lee Tunnel off Highway 81.

What comes back are their blue coveralls,
And how they hung their heads when their foreman,
The one they called Mr. J. D., seethed at them —

Perk up you bunch of goddamn sissy fusses and wipe off
Your grubby hands before you touch anything.

And maybe this is a story told best by hands:

The sales clerk twisting her pencil; my mother
Clutching her purse, squeezing my arm

Tighter and tighter; the security guard tapping
The handle of his blackjack.

Each man's hands with their fingerprints and palmprints,
Their sheen of salt and oil, cupping
The hem of a silk negligee, stroking the collar of a wool coat.

And one hand ghosting against the warm glass,
The white light of the jewelry counter,
Reminded me of a bird,
                          its delicate hinges and slender bones.

                    ::

Defeat brindles on the crows' calls, snags
In the thick scumble of pines.

It shakes itself from the green needles, a poison
Tunneling through snow,
                          sifting through a mizzle of sleet.

It's the knifelight in the water moccasin's eye.
It's an absence, a presence, siltslide and cutbank
Where the rhododendron roots fray mid-air.

Gauze and black sticks, halo of coal dust,
It drowns the poor in the backwater,
                              in the whiskeylight of winter.

Defeat unscrolls like a scrawl of smoke,
It slurs and spiders in the dark: fractured prayers
Blistering like headlights on icy asphalt.

::

I remember my grandmother — a neat woman,
A kind woman, a staunch Christian —

Looking out the picture window in her apartment
On the hill, a little tatter of Kleenex
In her fist, her lips pursed as she looked down

On the rooftops of the projects, the mildewed brick

And scraps of tarpaper lifting in the wind.

She turned to me and said, *The colereds ruin everything*
    they touch.
She said, *You watch who you make friends with, you hear?*

And I did hear, and heard again, a little later,
When she asked me over my cheese and juice,
Do you think if you died tonight you'd go to Heaven?

Later, when I lay in bed fearing an end
I couldn't even imagine, I gave God a body
And a name, and tried to pray:

I'm an honest boy, Hoss.
My heart is clay, Hoss.
O please Hoss, hollow me out before they do.

:::

Who is it that saunters there on State Street, holding his hat
With one chalky hand, flashing his polished flask in the other?

Brother Defeat in his swank suit,
                          hankie sprouting like a little flame.

Brother Defeat in his starched shirt and his tie
Snug in its Windsor knot,
His skin cloyed with the scent of rotting gardenias,   : 35

Heading down to the corner of Has Been & Never Will Be,
Where Sisyphus —
                          hunched on his milk crate, polyester shoulders
Worn down to a sheen, pants too tight and riding up
Like a bad dream —
                          plays his broken accordion,
Busking for gum wrappers and pocket lint.

Of all his busted instruments, he loves the accordion
The most, loves its duct-tape suture and the grooves
Fingered out on the whalebone buttons,

Loves the mice shit rattling around inside it.

Brother Defeat leans against the lamp post, tapping his foot
And stroking his white beard, tossing cashews to the crows

As Sisyphus, eyes shut tight, feels the mountain
Crumbling on his back, feels the night
Sweat through his three-piece suit,

And leans into his wheezing skeleton of song.

::

Because I wanted to believe in something,
I took the mountain inside me.

Because I believed it couldn't be moved,
I thought it wouldn't betray me.

It's the oldest story I know

But now a hole unfurls through it, through you,
Hoss, to the golf course and the country club,

And now you're nothing but the lost geography
Of the soul, not the place but the ideal of the place,

Some old longing, unattainable.

::

Once, God was the land without end,
And those at one with the land

Were at one with God, and work was not work
But a type of prayer, the sun warm on your neck,
The breeze blowing right through you

As your soul stepped out and ran ahead a little
Through the high grasses, through the tangled swell
Of woodbine and buckthorn, through the pines
Beyond the rimrock, and the mountain,

Which was the slow revelation of time itself.   : 37

Each thing the soul passed through left its outline,
Left its impression, like a wet feather plastered on glass.

It's one truth I know older than crows,
But it's been mapped, cut up, divvied out

So many times, it's worth nothing more now
Than the broken Christmas ornament
Strewn across the sidewalk as it begins to snow,

And Sisyphus shuffles back onto the bus
For the long ride back to the Get By.

It's too late for him now, but for a moment
Let me become part of each thing he knows—

Part of the snow planing down, then blown
Into waves of static. Part of the gold glass in the gutter,
The faint light locked behind each piece.

Part of the stray dog trotting around the corner
And its teats trotting in the air beneath it.

Part of the sighs the mountain swallows
And will not fling back.

Part of the sky that unfurls when he cradles
His head in his hands. Part of the crows that strut there.

Part of the watch ticking in his pocket and growing louder,

Time no longer contained but unbridled, one end of his-
Story folding over onto the other,

Endlessly, the way each thin flame of a fire
Lays down on the next, until what's left

Is the color of defeat, and weighs nothing.

::

I don't know what set the crows going, shovel-thump
Or shotgun, or perhaps the kiss of flint in the backs of
    their minds,
The way the snow kissed the asphalt, and the asphalt
    snuffed it out.

I don't know what it was, but one evening they disappeared.
Not for good at first, but they ended up
Where they were for a reason:

                there at Carter's Crossing,
On the hill behind the construction company, the dead burr oak
Alive now with their shifting and preening, their smoky skirls.   : *39*

Fire on the mountain, fire in the heart
And all those eyes flecked with gold

As Little Jimmy, and the one they called Mr. J.D.,
And Red the security guard from the store,
Stumbled from a pick-up, tossing the tarp off the back
Where Sisyphus was bound and gagged
For a watch lifted from beneath the glass.

They only meant to teach him a lesson, they said,

Until the shotgun was fumbled, snub-nose
Down, into the blue-black whump and nightsuck—

And this is where the story swirls and drifts, where I lose my
    place
For the watch has quit ticking and the men have stepped
    into the trees
As if stepping backstage, another act done, the theater dark
    and quiet
And filling with snow.

Sisyphus is curled where the spotlight once was, his mask
Peeled back to the face of a man, the wound beneath his eye
A wilted flower he's already become,

Just as he's become the clods of dirt that dribbled
Down his back, and the sound of cars siphoning from one side
To the next, the sweep and bounce of their headlights—

A man becoming something flawless
And iridescent, like the neck of a crow in a family of crows,
Or their measured slap of wings,
                            first one, then another,
Then all of them lifting through the molten smalt of memory,
Undulating, as if each bird was of one mind,
    was a single feather
On some larger bird,
                    emptied of flight one more time.

::

One by one, the men vanished into the landscape,

And the children returned to their desks,
Only to cradle their heads in their arms and forget
And drift, for good, out of the story into the chatter
And laughter echoing through the corridor.

How can I get it right? How can I push the pieces
Back into place now that the classroom has emptied

And dead leaves flutter in the coat closet,
Now that all the textbooks have filled with flames?

Tonight, my remembering is nothing more
Than a record of my forgetting, and the boy is where
I left him, alone, a blurry face at the window,

Waving now to the white men, comical in their pointy hats,
Now to the black men on the bus, their heads
Bowed, their shoulders slumped to the arc of the sledge.

I am him and not him, trembling in the air
Around his body as the snow
Exhausts its options against the glass.

I am him and not him, the crows long gone,
The day's lesson done and streaked across the blackboard,

A word that weighed nothing more than the lace handkerchief

Mrs. Rutherford coughed into,
Until the cough, or the memory of the cough, is all
I remember, all the truth has become,

A warm mist where a body once stood.

STILL LIFE WITH
CHARLIE & SHORTY

Whenever I see a barber's pole,
I think of the autumn of 1979
when Charlie Chandler hobbled
into Shorty Blevins' little shop
in Bristol, Virginia.

You know the type of place.
Springy vinyl seats and dog-eared
magazines piled on milk crates.
The walls cluttered with fishing trip
snapshots and Nascar glossies.

Broken bowling trophies,
an old mechanical soda machine,
and a handslap of frosty tonic
hanging on in the cigarsmoke.
I sat there with my father

every other Friday afternoon,
eating Cheetos, waiting my turn,
the politics and jokes lost on me.
O sweet nostalgia, you think.
O small town America,

O baseball and apple pie.
But no. Please. This is about
Charlie Chandler, five-foot-two
with a medicine ball belly.
How he groaned in pain

while Shorty leveled his flat-top,
muttering about that son-of-a-bitch
Mack Stigall at the packaging plant,
who'd unhooked a frozen cow
carcass onto his big toe.

And this is about Shorty Blevins,
how he hardly said anything,
working his clippers from the midst
of some vast silence, gazing
into your hair the way a man,

out-of-luck and lost,
stands in a ditch in the cold,
head tilted back, staring up
at the endless rainy night, waiting
for one goddamn sign.

What's the point of all this?
you ask. Who knows for sure.
Perhaps it's about memory,
how I can close my eyes and see
Shorty kneeling in front of the chair,

unlacing Charlie's shoe, sliding it
carefully off. The sock next, rolled
down over his thick, varicose ankle,
over his talcum-white foot,
and then folded into a precise square.

Perhaps it's about human ingenuity,
Shorty fishing a pen-knife
from his pocket, and the men
leaving their checkers and papers
to huddle around, leaning in,

steadied by canes or the shoulder
next to theirs, rheumy eyes
wide, stubbly jaws dropped in astonishment.
What would you think, stranger,
if while passing through town,

selling vacuums or life insurance,
you decided to stop in for a shave
and stumbled upon these men,
who don't even look up now
to nod in acknowledgment?

Let the boy lead you by the hand
close enough to see that this
is not some trick of light or mirrors:
real men, a real foot cradled
in a real hand, the toe blue-black

and swollen, the slender blade poised,
ready to drill through the dying nail
to let the trapped blood out.
All of it arrested in time, as if
you'd been swept into a painting

that had nothing and everything
to do with you, and when you open
your mouth to object, they all
vanish: Charlie into the rocky hills
of his childhood; Shorty into the blue

antiseptic silence of his scissors;
and each man into wind or paper
or fire, as the late sun seeps
through the blinds, the fulcrums
of amber light swimming

with dander and bits of hair.

::

For Charlie Chandler

MUSKRAT GOSPEL

As the banks go broke and the mines shut down,
    as the lumber mills close their doors
and the saw hum sinks into memory, into dirt and root
    and sap, my grandfather's body
begins to return to light. He's barely eighteen,

just married, jobless, and he's been trapping muskrats
    for months now just to get by,
and I know if I want to understand, I must wade
    into the cold creek at dusk
and look over his shoulder. The traps

have been boiled and waxed and blackened
    with crushed walnut hulls
and are slung across his back in a soft calfskin satchel,
    and I can tell by the way
he leans forward slightly, watching the fading sun

smudge the treetops into a scumble of gold,
    by the way he scouts the banks
for sodden furrows, for rifled bulrush and sweet flag,
    for shoddy dens of cattails and mud,
that he's eaten nearly nothing in a week.

He goes to work, baiting the pipes, wiring the traps,
    and if I want to understand,

I must follow him back before dawn when the jostle
    of his lantern sets them off,
the racket of their wrest and skirl spilling over

the cutbank into the dark. I must place my hands
    on his when he holds his breath
and cracks their velvet necks. Soon he'll dream
    they come for him, crawling
over his body, their chestnut pelts sliding across

his skin like a code of silk. This is not revenge,
    nor punishment, but a calling,
and their scent swamps him and he sleepwalks
    the cold creekbreak,
his feet slipping, his ankles buckling on the rocks.   *: 49*

When he wakes from the dream for the last time,
    he's diabetic, senile, a widower
stumped about how he's ended up in the dim-lit attic.
    It's past midnight, and he sits
unpacking a trunk, recognizing the smell that lifts

and hangs in the rafters for what it is — the smell of work
    and sex, of dirt, of music, of birth —
and he shudders with the sudden urge to undress.
    Earthly apparition, his flesh tinged
the opaque blue of milkglass, he peers into the trunk

as if it were a portal he might step through
    back into his youth, a blackness

that might give way to the gleam of a midnight
    blue Buick's polished paint
and chrome, to him and his wife ambling by

up State Street, their laughter amplified by the blaze
    of gas street lamps on snow.
Ambling, arm-in-arm, his cheap Fedora
    in a gambler's tilt,
and her homemade stole drawn

tightly beneath her chin. Ambling to the theater,
    this their honeymoon, a double-feature
where John Wayne with swagger and sweat will single-handedly
    defend the American Dream,
and Greta Garbo with one sultry glance will melt

their inhibitions like beeswax, their bodies
    becoming otherworldly
beneath the other's touch. They will forget cold cornmeal
    and bone-weary work, coal dust
and the caustic winter air; forget, as they pause to admire

the Buick, arm-in-arm, him gesturing confidently
    with his free hand, their reflections
sharp and translucent in the driver's side window,
    posed there in the glass.
And now he reaches in and sets it all in motion,

pulling up her old stole, rubbing it over his palms
    and face as if grace or mercy

might be conjured like an oil from its skin,
    draping it across his shoulders
and hobbling out of the house like a lost god

wandered off the silver screen. Old man,
    help me to understand.
Let me walk with you past the shuttered homes
    to where the oaks bank
against the night like a burned out marquee.

Show me the way, the path overgrown
    with bindweed and nettles.
Let me believe when I see you return
    to light and rise
to where the night's spindrift smolders

like bonemeal, to where the moon hangs,
    cold pendulum, still breath
of the dead. Ablution of light, light begetting light:
    let me believe it when I see you
fall again, laddering over black branches

into the creek, ocean bound, blood bound,
    sliding past where everything
bright-eyed and furred dreams in the dark, and grief
    lifts weightlessly from the backs
of the dying, wafting up like a familiar perfume.

::

Dedicated to the memory of my grandfather, Jack W. Lowe

MOCKINGBIRD GOSPEL

Consider this tiny scapula
staked in the dirt, all that's left

of a mockingbird struck down
by one thing or another,

sun-blanched, wind-scoured, pilfered
by buzzards, this miniature

bridge of bone the fire ants forage.
Who sings the songs it sang

beneath feather and flesh, its tongs
humming, a tuning fork struck

with breath and blood?
Let the boy come, fossicker of charms,

his pockets stuffed with jackstraws,
snakeskins, oxidized coins.

Let him pick it up and wish on it,
let him sing to this cipher

of calcium, this talisman of salt.
Let him place it under his pillow

where it divines the night —
umber from plum, plum from umber.

Grant it the strength to buttress
his weary head, to be a sled of white light

drawing him across fields of sleep.
And the crickets purl in the hedge.

And the owl flutes down its one note.
And soon he believes he no longer

needs it, flings it sidearm, boomerang
of bone, back into the field

where the sun fires its phosphor
and the rain fills its pores,

where the horses pulverize it to dust
and the wind scatters it in the bull-thistle.

And consider him now, fourteen,
naked, a little drunk, caught

in the snare of a dog-dare, he stands
on a sooty trestle, the river

spreading beneath him like creosote.
It's there on the water, the moon

grafting cradles of light. It's there
at the back of his throat, a fleck of feldspar

burning on his tongue. It's there
in gravity unsnagged, in the rush

of slow somersaults, in the hollow
swoon swanning in his gut.

He should be singing.
He should be singing for its touch:

a wing of blind grace, a finger of dumb luck.

NIGHT FISHING

– for my father

Duskshade. Nighthawks choreographing
their mad waltz along the tree line.
The jostle of mud turtles in the cattails.

Frog-bark and cricket-chatter. Mallards
drifting to the mouth of the creek,
the current coasting them back.

This is what stuck when the dark
dropped its anchor, and the lake lay
moon-skimmed and still in its socket.

We sat for hours, casting and recasting
our lines like translucent antennas.
Ten years old, I shunned sleep, giddy

with each distant plop of bait, each nibble
and tug. Most nights, we didn't catch
a single fish, and I couldn't understand

your calm, how you could hum your hymns
while the perch surfaced in defiance,
slapping their tails against the water.

Tonight, alone, much is the same:
moths bang against the tallowed lantern globe,
silver minnow-darts skirt the bank.

The mallards are still coasting.
I've returned for the mystery of it all,
but see, instead, what you saw too clearly:

The way we sway in isolated stations
with our burdens to bear. How the stars
like hammered sequins can lure a man,

and the barbed moon drag him down.

HALF-LIGHT

I remember the room in which my father
and I spent Saturday afternoons alone:
brown shag carpet, a La-Z-Boy, a tweed
sofa the color of rust, and a fireplace
full of soot, half-burnt logs, cold ash.
This the room where men could be men
after the day's work was done,
and my mother and sister had left us
to go shopping. We took off our shoes
and watched television until my father
removed his glasses, laid down his pipe,
and pushed the polished coffee table
out of the way. Down on all fours,
I was sure I could take him. We wrestled
until he'd had enough and pinned me
on my belly, rubbing his unshaven chin
against my cheek, poking me
in the side until laughter squeezed
my breath in two. Afterwards,
he taught me what I needed to know.
Once, it was how to shake hands firmly
and look a man straight in the eyes,
for this, he said, was the simplest measure
of honor and character. He made me
practice, my hand lost in his bear paw,
my name an odd language it seemed
I'd never spoken, as I introduced myself
to him, over and over, until he smiled
and nodded and said I was good.

While he napped on the sofa,
I lay on the floor and drew with crayons.
First, a picture of Jesus shaking hands
with Ronald Reagan, and next my father
shaking hands with a bear. And you might
shake your head and laugh and say
what an imagination I possessed at nine,
if I weren't looking you in the eyes now
to tell you how serious I was,
how I paused occasionally to study
my father's hands folded over his chest,
or to practice shaking hands with myself,
or to watch a man with iron fists boxing
on the television — tiny Ray "Boom Boom"

Mancini, lifting his opponent off his feet
with punches to the heart, before tangling
him in the ropes, sprawling him
across the canvas in the eighth round,
bloody and dying as the crowd roared —.
Yet all of this was long ago. Long before
I learned to anticipate the cool dusk,
the half-light of October, the shadows
of the firs cast in long spires across the lawn.
Long before the phone rang calling my father
to his father's death, and he stepped
over me to answer it. Long before I learned
to hug a man, his head in his hands,
his hair smelling of tobacco and tweed,
as the news sank in and the blue star
fuzzed out on our old television.

SELF-PORTRAIT WITH EINSTEIN'S TESTICLES

Early evening, and the winter dark
has already battened down

the rooftops of the farmhouses.
On the news, Walter Cronkite

drones on, some controversy
over Einstein's brain. I am eight.

I think Cronkite is British.
I think Einstein invented electricity,

his white coif singed, teased up
permanently from shocks and jolts

endured in the name of progress.
How I want this, my gangly body

to be a conduit for something
magnanimous, monumental,

and giddied by the idea, I dance around
my father splayed in his La-Z-Boy,

wagging my index finger
in the air, singing "Eureeeeka!"

to the beat of a saucy rumba.
I am too much, my mother says,

and sends me to the mudroom
to fold laundry. Instead,

I grab two light bulbs
off the shelf, and still breathless,

shake them like maracas, gyrating
my skinny hips. Then,

in my only stroke of genius,
I dangle them, giggling, between my legs,

stand there at the back of the house
in the dark, waiting for someone

to flip the switch, for the first light
to flicker, and flare on.

GOSPEL WITH SWINE & FIRE

How many times have you begun there —
Friday night on the outskirts of town,
where a dirt road meets a dilapidated bridge,
where a boy and a girl in the backseat of a borrowed car
lean into each other, all elbows and thumbs?
How often have you dreamed of them
and of the train that snakes through the dark distance,
the conductor half-asleep, humming?
Child of cold romance, child of white lies,
step onto the tracks into the brake screech
and the slatted cars packed with swine,
buckling and skidding into a field of ripe corn.
Child of smoke and crushed copper, carry your lantern
away from the others as they stumble out
in night clothes to gawk at the squealing freight —
some mangled and dazed, some hobbling about,
rooting in the furrows for a bit of corn.
You won't find what you're looking for there;
the boy and the girl have burnt out now
in the sputter of a blow torch, now in the cicada-whir,
now in the dashboard's green glow.
No. Your story is more ash than flame,
and begins here with your father
undressing in the dark, thirty-three years old
and sucking in his paunch, his thick horn-rimmed glasses
cocked on his nose, his white legs mapped by bluing veins.

It begins with your mother robed in a cotton gown,
flushed in the heat, her chapped hands smoothing
the blanket she's drawn up under her chin.
And there are no pigs, unless you consider
the meal they ate earlier — baked pork chops
with bread and butter and mashed potatoes —
and the train that passes through the foothills each night
when they lay down beside one another,
does so again without incident. Confess,
you are no accident, and there is no fire at all
but the God they fear burning in their hearts
as they tremble and reach across the dark.
It's so simple you can tell it no other way.
They close their eyes. They touch each other.

Their mouths are open in praise.

MONKEY GOSPEL FLOATING OUT TO SEA

Now that the boardwalk's been abandoned, and the pier's
Rotted and slumped into the sea,
                                    into the cold

We've all mucked through once,
Going nowhere, our pockets turned inside out,
Our rants trailing off in a line of bubbles—

Now that the voodoo candles in the windows
Of the mobile homes have guttered out,

And my childhood has gone up in a thin swirl of greasy smoke,

I will conjure happiness out of spindrift and salt air,
Out of wind, out of blown sand, out of the frail cries of
     the sparrows

Who nest at last in the white scaffolding
Of a forgotten roller coaster.

In 1980 I was seven and knew nothing
About the economics of risk or the risk of economics.

Hope burned in the long rows of colored lights, jangled
In the carousel's music, in the sirens wailing from the arcade.

Happiness was mine to win
                if my poise was steady enough,
If my thought was pure enough, if Lady Luck would bless
My good right eye and my aim

The way she blessed our old Ford
That smoked and rattled the whole nine-hour trip
To the beach, my father's knuckles white on the wheel,
His face in a rapt concentration that wooed her, I believed,

To keep the fire and grease in place,
To keep the wheels singing beneath us.

And when I bent to the floating bulls'-eyes
In the shooting gallery on the boardwalk in Myrtle Beach,   : *65*
He leaned over my shoulder,
               his breath fluttering behind my ear,

His face floating now, floating then
A target in its own way

That I did not understand, for I understood nothing
But the easy calculus of consequence:

Ping—
    the cowboy's hat spins and smokes.

Ping—
    the yellow mannequin herks and jerks over the player piano.

Ping—

    the stuffed monkey grins and stomps and clangs

      his cymbals together

        into the invisible

          shimmering brass body of glee.

    ::

Happiness was the music of space once,

On the boardwalk, when the organ grinder
In a red uniform with brass buttons
Churned his box of stars,
As his spider monkey, Milo the Great, turned flips
And walked on his hands, danced a little soft-shoe
And doffed his soiled hat so each child
Could toss in a coin or two.

Once I dreamt of it every night for a week,
Until the dream became so vivid
I could see, even after I woke, the man's buttons
Gleaming in their orbits,
And the tiny wrinkled hands of the monkey
That rode his shoulder, and could hear the music
Tinkling above the drone of the sea,
And felt my father's breath

      fluttering behind my ear.

But no matter how hard I tried, my father's breath
Grew cold and receded, and the music
Receded and fell like windchimes blown
Down into sand, and the monkey grew thin,
First on the man's shoulder and then in pure air,
Grew thinner and thinner until it was the dark itself

That shifted shape and followed me everywhere,
And would not recede.

::

In 1986, when I was thirteen, *Recession*
Was a word I knew.

That was the year my father lost his job
And stumbled home with a migraine and collapsed
In his La-Z-Boy, his eyes clamped shut.

There in the blankness that was his life and no one else's,
He saw it blow past him —

                                   a small, white thing
Like a hot dog wrapper stuttering end-over-end
Down the beach, lifting in the wind, falling, gone.

That was the year he and my mother sat up together
Late into the night, huddled at the kitchen table
Over the classifieds or scribbled figures,

As I slept in the next room, my body growing
Up around me like a tree that I looked out from,
The world happening without me for the first time,

The dark-that-would-not-recede perched on my shoulder,

The dark that I could not train, could not whip
Back into the shape of its beginning.

How I ended up that year dancing the last dance
Of the Spring Fling with Isis Castanata,
Who was half-deaf and had a weak heart,

How I ended up dancing with a girl who had
The beauty of a leaf glimpsed mid-fall, a beauty
Too sophisticated for adolescence, I do not know.

But we danced our bodies into one body,
                                        for just a moment, turning
In crooked, rhythmless circles like a maimed pelican
That can't make it back to shore.

                        ::

Happiness was a fistful of coins, or an animal—
Us but not us—its movements
Quick and comical, its palm the skin of a dried fig.

Happiness was not its eyes, which were
Emptiness, which held sadness like the sea at night,

The mouth that would not stop calling
To the boy and girl dancing, stumbling through the hot gym.

Happiness might be mistaken for the dancing,
For being held close by another,

But never for the sea, or how such a dark thing
Could toss light up through the slats of the floor.

::

When my father collapsed into his life,

Bedtime for Bonzo was halfway through
The eleventh hour of a twenty-four hour marathon,
And Reagan was well into the second year of his second term.

Voodoo Economics was a phrase I knew and *New World Order*
Meant no one knew exactly

How many people had to be mangled or bludgeoned
And bulldozed into mass graves,
Because they smelled and had faces shaped like monkeys',

Before someone made a motion
To make a motion that someone should do something.

The whole world was receding, vanishing
One plank of wood at a time, the pier, the boardwalk,
The arcade riding out the black tide.

The music, the buttons, the monkey, the television
With Bonzo looping without end, my father
Floating off in his chair with his pockets turned inside-out

And sinking, and Isis Castanata clinging to a branch

And sinking.

::

70 :   Our whole lives are quest and quest, I think.

A familiar face glimpsed on a busy street, then gone.
A name that can't find its groove on the tongue.

The faint, fleeting remembrance of another's touch,
A body of sunlight and air, or a cotton dress after the
    body vanishes.

Happiness stretches on that thin wire of shadow
Between sea and sky.

We want to pluck it, to hear its music sift up through
    the static,
But it keeps moving out.

Just like these sentences pushing out and out,
Face, name, body
                    then ending.

Just like when Jim Beaudoin and I
Reclined against a hawser coil once, there
Where the beached catamarans—sailless and sand-whipped—
Stooped in their sad rows. We swigged something
Cheap and quick, watching smoke from fireworks drift

Over blackwater, then break up and disappear
Into the spaces between the stars.

It all breaks up: my father's breath when I turn around
To meet it, her blue lips when I lean in to kiss them,
The monkey's face when I kneel to look at its eyes—.

                    ::

Isis Castanata, where are you now?

I've listened for your name on planes and in cafes,
In music drifting down from rooftops.
I've looked for your face in the wet eyes of animals,
In storefront reflections in every city and town.

I've searched and searched, and if I ran into you today
Wandering the stacks in the library, I imagine,
The day beyond the high windows clear blue and leaf-blown,

I would tell you what I've never told anyone.
How your shoulder blades beneath your thin dress.
Felt like the stumps of wings.

How your bad heart fluttered between us
Like a sparrow cupped between two hands.

How happiness slipped into the world once
On the back of an animal

And climbed into this poem when I least expected it,
Translucent and hollow-boned, veined like a leaf.

It fluttered and brushed against us and couldn't be held.

It flutters and brushes against me and can't be held.

::

And this is what I remember now, when the smell of the sea
Is the smell of hair, breath, skin,

When I can find the courage and the right chord
To coax the dark down from its high branch,
And cradle it, just for a moment.

In my arms it might find the shape of a dying animal,
Us but not us, its eyes wet with the sea,
And I float there in them.

Banked behind me is not art, nor fire, nor language,
But a buckling boardwalk and boarded up arcade,
Broken bulbs and a busted pumpbox of fog.

Quest and quest, and step out of it.

I lay it down in the sand covering my feet,
I lay it down where the tide will carry it out

And step out of it,
Into the here and now far from the sea,
Into the middle of the country, into the middle of a life

That is mine to snatch up and keep.

: *73*

Outside the world is dying, full burn, the day
A rain of leaves. By the kitchen window,
The feeder's a flurry of chickadees and tit mice,
Woodpeckers and sparrows.

Later I will speak with my father on the phone.
Familiar jokes, familiar reservation,
But his breath, his voice on the other end
Uncertain, a honeycomb of rust.

Happiness is so close in my house, so close
It flutters, it gathers loss up into a body of salt.

My wife is curled up on the couch with a book,
A good wool sweater and thick socks, a cup of tea
Sending up its flags of steam.

And when dusk starts to charcoal the windows,
I know that somewhere
Pierlights are flickering on in their wire baskets,

That the moment is already wandering
       the distance of night, stars, sleep.

I hold her and close my eyes and smell the woodsmoke
In her hair, and try to feel every atom
Swimming in the heat between us.

I try to hold it, the hum, the burn —.

ACKNOWLEDGEMENTS

My gratitude to the editors of the following journals where poems in this collection first appeared, sometimes in different versions:

Bellingham Review, "Elegy with a Mute Bell"

Blackbird, "Flood"

The Indiana Review, "Self-Portrait with Einstein's Testicles"

Painted Bride Quarterly, "Crow Gospel Coming Down from the Mountain"

Pleiades, "Snow Over Shavers Fork"

Poetry, "Dog Gospel"

Quarterly West, "Still Life with Charlie and Shorty," "Guinea Pig Gospel," "Self-Portrait with a Burnt Out Light Bulb"

River Styx, "Muskrat Gospel"

Sou'wester, "The Trees of the South"

The Texas Review, "Mockingbird Gospel"

"Dog Gospel" received "Special Mention" in the 2006 *Pushcart Prize XXX: The Best of the Small Presses.*

"Flood," "Dog Gospel," and "Crow Gospel Coming Down from the Mountain" were runners-up in the 2005 Campbell Corner Poetry Prize.

Many thanks to my teachers—Greg Donovan, Mark Doty, Edward Hirsch, Eric Pankey, and Adam Zagajewski. I owe each of you a deep debt of gratitude for showing me the way.

Thanks also to the following writers and friends for their invaluable advice, wisdom, and encouragement: Nicky Beer, Jay Bridgers, Murray Farish, Steve Fitzpatrick, Jennifer Grotz, Sean Hill, Lynne McMahon, Wayne Miller, Lee Newton, Todd Samuelson, and Sherod Santos.

I am grateful to Inprint, Inc. for a C. Glenn Cambor Fellowship that supported the writing of these poems.

To my parents, for their love and support: I am eternally grateful.

And finally, to Nicky: I owe you everything.